bubblefacts...
VIKING INVADERS

Miles Kelly
PUBLISHING

First published in 2005 by
Miles Kelly Publishing Ltd
Bardfield Centre, Great Bardfield, Essex, CM7 4SL

Copyright © Miles Kelly Publishing Ltd 2005

2 4 6 8 10 9 7 5 3 1

Editorial Director:
Anne Marshall

Senior Editor:
Belinda Gallagher

Editorial Assistant:
Hannah Todd

Designer:
Louisa Leitao

Cartoons:
Mark Davis

Production:
Estela Boulton

ISBN 1-84236-535-5

Printed in China

British Library Cataloguing-in-Publication Data
A catalogue record for this book is available from the British Library

Indexer: Jane Parker

www.mileskelly.net
info@mileskelly.net

Contents

Kings and people

Vikings rule!

The Vikings lived in Scandinavia more than 1000 years ago. They spread terror throughout Europe between AD800 and 1100. Viking warriors made fierce raids on peaceful villages, battled to win new land, plundered treasures and snatched people to sell as slaves.

DARNED FISH ARE TOO QUICK!

NO TA, I'M ON A DIET!

WELL IF YOU DON'T WANT IT...

mmm I WILL!

WHAT D'YOU FANCY FOR SUPPER? CHINESE?

OH! STOP PRETENDING!

Slaves, farmers and warriors all worked hard. King Erik Bloodaxe killed his brothers so he could be king.

At the top of Viking society were nobles (kings or chiefs). They were rich and had many servants. The middle group included farmers and craftworkers. Slaves were the lowest group. They worked hard for nobles and could not leave their owner.

Viking rulers had strange names such as Svein Forkbeard, Thorfinn Skullsplitter and Sigurd the stout.

King Bluetooth built a memorial for his family. King Cnut tried to command the waves – and failed!

Sailors and raiders

row your boat

Vikings sailed in dragon ships.

Cargo ships were slow and heavy, with wide, deep hulls to carry loads. Ferry and river boats were small and sturdy. The most splendid ships were drakkar (dragon ships), designed for war. They were long, slender and speedy, with beautifully carved sterns and prows.

Dragon ships had shallow keels that enabled the Vikings to sail quickly onto beaches to make raids.

Vikings liked living in longhouses, because heat from the animals provided a kind of central heating, keeping them warm.

Viking pirates such as King Svein Forkbeard of Denmark (ruled AD985-1014) demanded money from the English. He led Viking warships to England and promised to attack if he was not paid to sail away. Svein's tactics worked. Each time he returned, the English handed over 'Dane-geld' (gold for the Danes) – again and again!

AATCHOO! BLESS ME.

TIMBER! THERE SHE GOES, LADS.

SNAP!

CRASH

EEK!

Tall trees provided long planks for ships. Vikings used overlapping planks of ash, oak or birch for the hull.

Warriors and weapons
going beserk!

Vikings valued glory over long life. They believed that a dead warrior's fame lived on after him, and made sure that his name would never die. Myths and legends also told how warriors who died in battle would go to Valhalla, home of the gods, for a feasting banquet.

Berserkirs were fierce warriors who wore animal skins and charged at the enemy, howling like wolves.

Viking kings or lords led their followers into battle. Their men won praise for their loyalty.

Warrior spirits went to Valhalla, home of the gods. They named their swords and were buried with them.

Women and children
ruling the roost

Viking women were very independent. They made important household decisions, cooked, made clothes, raised children, organized slaves and managed farms and workshops while their husbands were away.

Women worked hard at looking after their families. Only widows could marry who they chose to.

After bathing, Vikings jumped into cold water. Warriors took their swords to the toilet for protection!

Warriors ate onions to diagnose stomach injuries. Long, flowing hair indicated a woman was unmarried.

Skilled craftworkers
tools of the trade

Vikings made most of the things they needed. Families had to make – and mend – almost everything – from their houses and furniture to farm carts, children's toys and clothes. They had no machines to help them, so most of this work was done slowly and carefully by hand.

Blacksmiths travelled around, making and mending tools. Bones were carved into combs by craftworkers.

To make a brooch, silversmiths hammered a die (a block of metal marked with a brooch design) into a sheet of silver. Then they added detail such as filigree (drops of molten silver) and nielo (a black paste).

Traders bought and sold goods using pieces of silver, which they weighed out on silver scales.

OH, YOU SHOULDN'T HAVE!

I DIDN'T!

I FEEL LIKE ONE OF THE SEVEN DWARFS!

BANG

Silversmiths made necklaces from twisted silver wires. Stoneworkers carved cups and bowls from cliffs.

Viking towns

getting settled

Kings built towns to encourage more trade. Before the Vikings grew so powerful, merchants traded at fairs held just once or twice a year. Viking kings built towns so that trade could continue all year round. Taxes were collected from the people and merchants who traded there.

CHAAARGE!

NOT ANOTHER DOOR TO DOOR SALESMAN!

POTS AND POTS... OF POTS!

OOH LOOK! HE'S POTTY!

Traders swapped goods, or paid for them using bits of silver, which were later developed into coins.

Towns were targets for attack. Pirates and raiders from Russia and north Germany sailed across the Baltic Sea to snatch valuable goods from Viking towns. So kings paid for towns to be defended with high banks of earth and strong wooden walls.

The name 'Russia' comes from the word 'Rus' used by people living east of the Baltic Sea to describe Viking settlers.

Space was limited inside town walls, which were defended by troops of warriors.

Vikings lived in a harsh environment, with cold, long, dark winters. Buildings were needed to shelter livestock, as well as people. In parts of the countryside, farmers built longhouses, with rooms for the family at one end and for animals at the other.

wooden rafters

outside lavatory

Houses did not have windows so were often full of smoke, making Vikings prone to chest diseases.

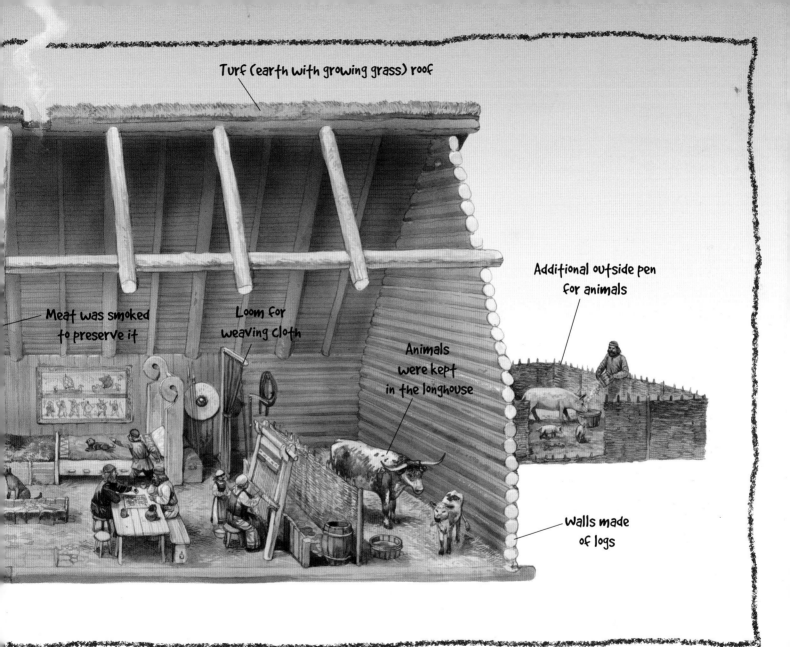

Turf (earth with growing grass) roof

Additional outside pen for animals

Meat was smoked to preserve it

Loom for weaving cloth

Animals were kept in the longhouse

Walls made of logs

Longhouses were built on sloping ground so that animal waste ran downhill, away from living areas.

Time for dinner

fun of the feast!

Vikings ate two meals a day. First thing in the morning was the 'day meal' of barley bread or oatcakes, butter or cheese. The main meal – 'night meal' – was eaten in the early evening. It included meat or fish, plus wild berries in summer. Meals were served on wooden plates or soapstone bowls and eaten with metal knives and wood or horn spoons.

Viking women and slaves cooked huge meals over open fires and served them to feasting warriors.

Red-hot stones boiled water for cooking. Few Viking homes had ovens so women and servants boiled meat in iron cauldrons. They also used water-filled pits that were heated by stones that had been placed in fire to make them red-hot. This was a very efficient way of cooking.

Feasts went on for a week or more. After winning a great victory, Vikings liked to celebrate. Kings and lords held feasts to reward their warriors, and families feasted at weddings. Guests dressed in their best clothes and hosts provided much food and drink. Everyone stayed in the feast hall until the food ran out, or they grew tired.

Viking warriors drank from curved cattle horns, but most people drank from wooden or pottery beakers.

Law and order

keeping the peace

Vikings followed a strict code of honour. Men and women were proud and dignified, and honour was important to them. It was a disgrace to be called a cheat or a coward, or to run away from a fight. Vikings also prized loyalty. They swore solemn promises to be faithful to lords and comrades and sealed bargains by shaking hands.

Quarrels were settled by fighting and this often lead to family feuds that lasted for months.

Viking laws were not written down. Instead, they were memorized by a man known as the law-speaker. He recited the laws out loud every year so that everyone could hear and understand them.

Every year Vikings met at the Thing – a gathering of all free men where they discussed punishments for prisoners.

GO ON, SHAKE ON IT...

HUMPH!

COME ON, LET'S ALL BE FRIENDS AGAIN.

...IT WAS THIS BIG! HONEST!

FOR MY NEXT TRICK...

Feuding families eventually had to call a truce. Viking thieves were hanged or outlawed.

Having a laugh

relaaax!

Vikings liked to have a good time. At feasts, people sang songs and danced. When relaxing, Vikings often played dice and board games. They loved playing practical jokes too, and listening to stories about gods and heroes who defeated enemies by trickery.

ALTOGETHER NOW!

SNIFF SNIFF!

MAY I HAVE THIS DANCE?

A Viking feast included lots of food, drink and dancing. A feast could go on for several days!

Vikings had a good sense of humour, and they liked jokes. In summer they played games and ran races.

Acrobats and jugglers were popular at feasts. Sports such as archery were good training for war.

Gods...
and goddesses

Viking people honoured many gods. The Aesir (sky gods) included Odin, Thor and Tyr, who were gods of war, and Loki, who was a trickster. The Vanir (gods of earth and water) included Njord (god of the sea) and Frey (the farmers' god). He and his sister Freyja brought pleasure and fertility.

Thor, god of thunder, travelled in a chariot pulled by goats. Odin god of war, rode an eight-legged horse.

The Vikings believed that they could win favours from the gods by offering them gifts. Since life was the most valuable gift, they gave the gods sacrifices of animals – and people.

one story told how Viking god Thor dressed up as a bride and pretended to marry a giant who had stolen his golden hammer.

WHAT A DRIP!

FREE ENTRY FOR SPIRITS!

VALHALLA HERE WE COME, BOYS!

Njord was the sea god. Warrior spirits went to live with the goddess Freyja, or Valhalla, home of the gods.

Death and burial

a good send off

The dead took useful items with them to the next world. The Vikings believed that peoples' souls survived to go on living in the next world. The bodies of the dead were surrounded by 'grave goods' – all kinds of things they might need such as clothes, weapons and jewellery.

I'M NO ANGEL!

SHE WAS SUCH A NICE LADY!

SNIFF!

A TRUE DIAMOND!

SNIFF

BUT THAT'S MY FAVOURITE SHIELD IN THERE, NOT HIS!

Vikings burned their dead on fires and collected the ashes. From AD800, unburned bodies were buried.

can you believe it?

Some Viking skeletons that were buried in acid soil have been eaten away but have left shadows in the ground.

Vikings treated dead bodies with respect. They washed them, dressed them and wrapped them in cloth or birch bark before burying them or cremating them. This was because the Vikings believed that dead people might come back to haunt them if they were not treated carefully.

BON VOYAGE!

RIGHT, I'M OFF BEFORE SEA-SICKNESS SETS IN!

Sometimes, the dead were laid to rest in cloth-covered shelters on board ships that were set on fire.

Kings defeated the Vikings.

For centuries, kings in England, Scotland and Ireland failed to drive the Vikings from their lands. But after AD1000, they began to succeed. Brian Boru, high king of Ireland, defeated the Vikings in 1014, and Viking rule ended in England in 1042.

In 1066 the Normans (descendants of Vikings) invaded from Normandy, France, and conquered England.

Vikings learned to live alongside other peoples. In most places where they settled, Vikings married local women and worked with local people. Some of their words and customs blended with local ones, but many simply disappeared.

After AD1000, Viking settlers landed in America, but the Native Americans drove them away.

Index